HOW TO PREPARE FOR HEAVEN

A Must Read for This Generation

Pastor Mike Chuks Nwanegbo

This book is dedicated to all those who aspire to make heaven at all cost. It is also dedicated to the brave men and women who had put their lives on the line in mission fields unlocking the gates of heaven for souls to gain access through the preaching of the gospel. You are all indeed God's fellow workmen. You shall all shine like stars. I want to appreciate my wife and children for going into the mission field with me. You too will shine like stars.

CONTENTS

Title Page	1
Dedication	3
Introduction	9
HEAVEN AT ALL COST	15
SIGNS OF THE END	18
WHAT HAPPENS WHEN WE DIE?	21
DOES HELL REALLY EXIST?	24
DOES HEAVEN EXIST?	27
THE VALUE OF HEAVEN	32
ABRAHAM AND THE FATHERS OF FAITH LOOKED TO HEAVEN AT ALL COST	36
HOW TO PREPARE FOR HEAVEN?	38
HOW TO SECURE YOUR ETERNITY	52
THE ROLE OF PARENTS IN PREPARING THEIR CHILDREN TO HEAVEN.	55
HOW TO BUILD TREASURES IN HEAVEN	58
THOSE WHO WILL NOT MAKE HEAVEN.	64
CAN THE DEVIL STOP YOU FROM PREPARING FOR HEAVEN.	68
CAN DELIVERANCE HELP PREPARE YOU FOR HEAVEN?	71
CAN you ENJOY HEAVEN WHILE ON EARTH?	76
About The Author	85

INTRODUCTION

I am always moved by the emptiness I sense in people as I interact with them in society. Several people seem lost. There is so much hustle and bustle. People desperately seeking material success at all cost. They cheat, sweat, kill and do all sort of things to achieve what they call success. The word "making it" is in the mouth of every one. The question is: what is "making it"? Some achieve so much fame and financial riches yet they seem the most miserable in life. After acquiring so much wealth, some just commit suicide after discovering that it is all vanity upon vanity.

So many want to make it to a place of material success but very few ever think of making it after life on earth. So many do not care about the life after here, but the truth is that it cannot be ignored. If you ignore it, it will not ignore you. Life on earth is like a drop on the ocean compared to life after death. Life after death is for ever and cannot change.

I hear of people preparing for retirement but very few are preparing for eternal retirement. The present illusion of life and ignorance of life after death has been deepened by some invisible hands to bring men to a place of eternal regret and shame.

In the western world the need for heaven is no longer an issue. It has been relegated to the background. This is a great injustice to our generation. So many people do not have a clue of life after death, not to talk of how to get there and how to secure their future in eternity.

In this book I have tried to the best of my ability to explain the

need to prepare for heaven and how to prepare and get to heaven. I have also tried to prove that you can start enjoying your heaven of earth while you wait for heaven in eternity. This part of the discuss will open your eyes to resources available to you to enjoy life on earth that most people have ignored.

I believe that by the time you are done with reading this book, your mind will be repositioned and you will no longer be afraid of death, but look to death as a transition to a better future in eternity.

It will also take you away from chasing the shadow of material wealth to building treasures in heaven for your eternal retirement.

If you buy into this reality, you will pursue heaven at all cost. It will become the ultimate and will change your perception of life on earth. One thing it will teach you is that there is nothing earthly worth dying for.

It will liberate you from the illusion of making money at all cost thereby releasing you to the real life on earth and a hope of eternal life in heaven.

Harvest of Nations

www.harvestofnations.org

HEAVEN AT ALL COST

Every human, who is truthful to self would agree that somewhere in his or her heart, is this desire for eternity. Eternity is in all our hearts. Atheists try to suppress this natural urge for life in eternity but the truth is that it cannot be suppressed.

This hidden desire to make heaven or urge to merge with God as some would call it, has led men into desperate search for the best way to attain peaceful eternity. Some have resorted to meditation, astral travel, penance, self-mutilation etc. Some have gone to the extent of trying to please God through martyrdom. Martyrdom has been defined differently by different people. Some religions believe that killing infidels would guarantee them a place in heaven. Some do believe that defending their faith by taking up arms would guarantee them a place in heaven. What a mystery? If men are so convinced that blowing up selves or defending their religious believe would guarantee them heaven, then this heaven must be so real and must be attained at all cost. In the days of the crusade young men flocked to join the crusade in other to defend their faith and many believed that their actions would guarantee them heaven. To most, defending the faith was not the real motive but making it to heaven.

In our present age so many young men are flocking to join militant group with the belief that they would make it to heaven if they die as martyrs. Governments had wondered what attracts so many young men to join these militant groups. The answer is simple; they are responding to the innate desire of man to find an easy way to making it to heaven. Research has proved that most people that claim to go to fight to defend their faith have little or no grasp of what their religious faith really teaches. To every human, there is that desire for heaven at all cost. Yes, heaven must be attained at all cost but how?

If there is heaven, how do we really get there and who will lead us to this eternal home that all humans yearn for? Most religions believe that heaven is the abode of God and going to heaven will mean going to meet God. If heaven is the abode of God, it means that only God can truly claim to know the right way to get to heaven.

Of all the so called gurus, prophets and masters, only one claimed to be the way and that one is Jesus Christ- (John 14:6.) He did not only claim to be the way but the only way. Others claimed to be looking for the way or claim to know the way. How can they know the way except God reveals it to them? Is Jesus really the only way to God?

I am fully convinced that Jesus is the only way. All religions somehow claim that God is Love. If God is love, it means that the best way to get to him is through love. Of all the prophets, gurus and masters, only one truly preached undiluted love. That one was Jesus Christ. Jesus commanded us to love our enemies, love our neighbours, pray for those that persecute and use us. (Matthew 5:44). Does this not sound like real love?

He commanded us not to curse, to turn the other cheek when we are hit on one cheek, to forgive so that we would be forgiven. He is the only one who boldly said that he is one with the father and that he came from the father. (John 10:30). If he is one with the father, it means that he also is love. To crown it all he was the only one who forgave sins and the forgiven felt forgiven immediately without doubt. (John 8:11). One thing that is amazing was that even demons confessed that he is the son of God.

"When He came to the other side into the country of the Gadarenes, two men who were demon-possessed met Him as they were coming out of the tombs. They were so extremely violent that no one could pass by that way. 29. And they cried out, saying, "What business do we have with each other, Son of God? Have You come here to torment us before the time?" Matthew 8:28-29.

"Before the time"? What time one would ask? It means that even the demons know that there is a set time and that time is the end of all men; when God will judge all. If there is judgement, then there will also be punishment and reward. The condemned are sent to hell and the acquitted are rewarded in heaven.

To crown it all, Jesus resurrected and ascended to heaven. Of all the prophets, gurus and masters ever known to mankind, no one was ever recorded as resurrecting from death, not to talk of ascending to heaven. It is worthy to note that he first descended to hell to set the captives free before ascending.

If Jesus ascended to heaven, it means that we must look at his teachings again. Apart from urging us to follow him to heaven, he warned that those who refuse to follow him will descend to hell. He warned that hell is a terrible place and that it would be better to enter into heaven with one arm cut than enter into hell full. (Mark 9: 45-47). What Jesus was saying is simply to make sure you make heaven at all cost.

My question to you today is: will you make it to heaven? Do not be deceived by your position in the church. Being a pastor cannot save you. Being a church goer cannot save you. Being a good person is not sufficient. Your righteousness is not sufficient to save you. What you need to be sure of salvation is to accept Jesus for real, obey his word and make sure you are quick to forgive. Live your life by the word and the spirit.

SIGNS OF THE END

The ice caps are melting; species are going extinct. Scientists estimate that about two hundred species are going extinct every 24 hours. (John Vidal 2011). The rain forest is being designated at remarkable rates. The consequences of genetically modified food are unknown; the earth is being robbed of its resources, oceans being poisoned by pollution. There is increasing global temperature. The earth is like an aging woman, unable to replenish self. The earth has been robbed of its strength. The earth is now hopeless and will someday die off.

The scientists are aware of this so they are looking for other sources of life in the Galaxies. This will not help issues because no matter what, death awaits

every living soul.

The Bible clearly point out that we are in the last days. It pointed out some signs we must watch out for. One thing is clear; these signs are here. Not only that the Bible talks about these signs, but also warns us to prepare for life after death, as the end of the world will usher us before the throne of God for judgment.

For me, the most authentic sign of the end time will be those mentioned by Jesus Christ Himself. The disciples of Jesus provoked Him to reveal to us the signs of the end time in Mathew 24:3.

" .... And what shall be the sign of thy coming and of the end of the world?"

This clearly means that the coming of Jesus Christ will really mean the end of the world.

"4 And Jesus answered and said unto them, Take heed that no man deceive you.

5. For many shall come in my name, saying, I am Christ; and shall deceive many.

6. And ye shall hear of wars and rumours of wars: see that ye be not troubled: for all these things must come to pass, but the end is not yet.

7. For nation shall rise against nation, and kingdom against kingdom: and there shall be famines, and pestilences, and earthquakes, in divers places.

8. All these are the beginning of sorrows.

9. Then shall they deliver you up to be afflicted, and shall kill you: and ye shall be hated of all nations for my name's sake.

10. And then shall many be offended, and shall betray one another, and shall hate one another.

11. And many false prophets shall rise, and shall deceive many.

12. And because iniquity shall abound, the love of many shall wax cold.

13. But he that shall endure unto the end, the same shall be saved.

14. And this gospel of the kingdom shall be preached in all the world for a witness unto all nations; and then shall the end come."

I will love to list out the signs one after the other:

1. Verse 5. Many will come clamming to be Christ.
2. Verse 6-7. There will be rumours of war and Nations shall rise against Nations, Kingdoms against Kingdoms, there shall be pestilences, famine and earthquake in diverse places.
3. Verse 9-10. Christians will be persecuted and hated of all Nations for the sake of the name of Jesus. Offence will come and they shall betray one another and shall hate one another.
4. False prophets shall rise and deceive many.
5. Iniquity will abound causing the love of many to grow cold.
6. The Gospel shall be preached in the entire world for a witness unto all Nations.

We can see that all the above mentioned are almost fulfilled. The happening of the above is enough evidence that Jesus is coming back and that the end is at hand. If the end is at hand, it means that heaven is at hand for those that have prepared for it.

If Jesus is coming again, then where had He been if not in Heaven? He said

"I go to prepare a place for you so that where I am you will also be" (John 14:2)

Apart from the fact that this earth will also wax old and be folded away, another reason why we must make Heaven at all cost is because if you miss Heaven, the only place left is Hell.

Whether we believe it or not, we must find out the truth at the end of life. Anybody who has not prepared for Heaven will regret at the end of life when they will suddenly discover that they had the opportunity to make heaven but ignored the great opportunity. They would cry for another chance but unfortunately there will be no other chance. It is now on earth that you have all the chances to prepare for heaven. There is no repentance and preparation in the grave. The signs of the end is here. It is better not to ignore this truth.

WHAT HAPPENS WHEN WE DIE?

Some religious groups simply believe in reincarnation. Reincarnation means coming back to life after death in another form. It could be in a lower life form or a superior life form depending on how you lived your previous life. Reincarnate is another way of saying there is life after death. The difference is that they believe you will come back to earth to begin another circle on earth. The Atheists say that there is no life after death. They claim that if you die, you are dead and that is it for you. It really does not make sense else there would be no need for life in the first place.

One thing is clear; every human being has eternity embedded in his or her heart. Some may ignore it but at the point of death, we all have questions and many are gripped by the fear of the unknown. When this earth passes away or when we pass away from this earth, where then do we go?

As a practicing Christian, I believe there is a place called Heaven. It is a place where those who accepted the covenant of God through Christ are preserved and rewarded. Some may have a different view but I would request that you reason a little with me for now.

Heaven is the abode of God. It is a place characterised by righteousness, peace and joy.

Reason here with me:

If a rapist and murderer rapes and kills innocent people, and is never caught by the law, do we conclude that such a one has gotten away free? Common sense tells us that there is always justice.

For such, where will justice be served? I am sure it must be after death.

The bible says that it is appointed unto man to die but once and after that judgement. (Hebrew 9:27). Life does not just end. Man must account for his actions on earth.

There is heaven and there is hell. Every soul will be brought to judgement after death and those who are found guilty are sent to eternal punishment in hell separated from the presence of God. While those who are found to have lived according to the ways of God are sent to heaven to live in eternal bliss.

How can one be innocent before God seeing that no man is good and that we are all sinners? This is one of the mysteries of God. God knows that no man is good and that all have sinned and come short of His glory. God knows that according to his law, no man will be able to get into heaven therefore eternal death await man in hell. The bible made it clear that it is not the will of God that anyone should perish, so God made heaven available to all men but man must choose by himself where to spend eternity. God has made this very easy by sending his son Jesus Christ to die in the place of man. Jesus died our death. His suffering and blood, was the appeasing sacrifice. It was a divine exchange. It was a covenant. By this covenant, anyone who accepts Jesus Christ as having paid for his or her sins and lives by his word is accepted and such a person's name is written in the book of life and acquitted at the court of judgement. It sounds so easy but that is the mystery of God. That is why it is called a free gift. The moment your name is written in the book of life; God gives you the grace to live a holy life but the choice must be yours to live such life or not. If you make a mistake and sin, and if you repent, the blood of Jesus is available to wash your sins. The moment you acknowledge your sins and repent; the blood of Jesus automatically washes your sins. The greatest sin is refusing to accept Jesus as God's redemptive sacrifice for us. By refusing Jesus, you have made God the father a liar. It means that you are telling God that you are good enough and that your righteousness is sufficient to earn you a place in heaven. God made it clear when he said that your righteousness is but a filthy rag before him. The bible says that those who refuse Jesus are already condemned. This also is a mystery.

If you continue to sin and refuse to turn from your sins, God will send several warnings through the word and through circumstances. If you refuse to repent and die in your sin, your name will be erased from the book of life and hell will definitely become your portion. I am not saying this to scare you but to warn you that there is judgement after death but through the covenant of the death and resurrection of Jesus, you can avert that Judgement and receive the grace to make heaven.

DOES HELL REALLY EXIST?

In my search on Google, I came across a definition which makes more sense to me. It defined hell as:

"A place referred in various religions as a spiritual realm of evil and suffering, often traditionally depicted as a place of perpetual fire beneath the earth where the wicked are punished after death".

Several people have given us testimonies of the existence of Hell. They have told horrible and fear gripping stories of Hell. One thing about Hell is that it is for ever and ever.

As usual with me, I would prefer to rely on Biblical information on Hell. The Bible has proven that it has never failed in its prophecies and information. Scientists have on several occasions got their clues from the Bible.

Rev 21:8 tells us that those who will have their place in Hell include:

"...the fearful, and unbelieving, and the abominable, and murderers and whoremongers, and sorcerers, idolaters, and all liars shall have their part in the lake which burneth with fire and brimstone: which is the second death."

Mathew 25:30 describes it as a place of gnashing of teeth. It is a place for unprofitable servants. I hear people say that a servant of God cannot go to Hell. The Bible says that unprofitable servants can be cast into Hell. (Matthew 25). If you are not winning souls or profiting the Kingdom of God in anyway, you stand a risk of being cast into Hell. This is not to scare you but to wake you up.

Mathew 22:13 calls it a place of outer darkness.

Luke 16:23 call it a place of torment. The torment in Hell cannot be compared to any Kind of torment on earth.

II Samuel 22:6 calls it a place of sorrow. No sorrow on earth can be compared to the sorrow of hell especially for those who profess to be Christians but lived in sin on earth. On getting to hell, they would find that they should have been in heaven. They will have the privilege of seeing heaven from hell. There will be great sorrow and regrets.

II Thessalonian 1:9 calls it a place of everlasting destruction.

Revelation 21:8 tells us that it is a place where men are tormented with fire and brimstone.

Mark 9:44 says that it is a place where the fire is not quenched.

Revelation 14:11 says it is a place where the inhabitants are tormented day and night without rest.

Anyone who receives the mark of the beast will never escape this eternal torment. Be warned. This book may fall into your hand when we the true Christians have raptured to be with Christ. At that time the man of sin called the anti-Christ will cause men to take his mark or be killed. It is better to die than take the mark of the beast. If you take the mark, you are dammed for ever. The mark of the beast is the number 666. Those who do not have the mark of the beast cannot buy nor sell.(.) Accept Christ today and prepare for heaven at all cost; even if it means suffering on earth. The suffering on earth cannot be compared to the glory of heaven. It is better you lose everything on earth and make it to heaven than gain everything and lose all in hell.

Revelation 20:14 call it a lake of fire.

Luke 16:24 calls it a place of hopelessness and taste. There will be no water to drink to quench taste.

One thing about Hell is that the pain never subsides and one cannot die. In Hell, one has full consciousness and memories. You will always wish you were in Heaven.

It will be worse for those who were Christians but played away their salvation.

Every day, thousands of people go to hell. Many will be shocked when they are sentenced to hell. They will just find out that they had the opportunity to avoid hell but they reasoned it off. They could not see how accepting Jesus could take them to Heaven. Some easily explain all happening scientifically. In hell, your science will be useless as you will not be able to explain scientifically what is happening to you.

Hell is not a place for any human. It was not created for human beings but for the devil and his agents. God never wills that any man should go to hell. Man goes to hell out of his own doing by freely or willingly rejecting God's offer for salvation, which is the acceptance of Jesus as our Saviour and our Lord. Hell is definitely not an option. It must be Heaven at all cost.

We must do all we can to make it to Heaven. Hell is a no go area for any soul. You do not want to end up in hell.

This reading will testify against you on the last day if you do not do anything about your soul today.

Two main things will for sure send a person to hell. The first is the refusal to accept Jesus as Lord and saviour. God has made him Lord and saviour of all souls. Refusing him means refusing God's offer of salvation for your soul. A soul that is not redeemed by the blood cannot inherit the kingdom of God and will have its place in hell.

The second thing that can send a soul to hell is living in sin. If one is redeemed but continues to live in sin without repenting, such a soul is making mockery of the redemptive blood of Christ. Hell for sure awaits such a one.

You shall be holy for the Lord thy God is Holy. 1 peter 1:16

DOES HEAVEN EXIST?

The Bible tells us of certain people that went to Heaven. Elijah was taken to Heaven in a chariot.

Many people claim to have had Heavenly encounter. Some claim they have been to Heaven and back. This we cannot verify but we can verify the account of Apostle John the beloved. The Lord Jesus ordered him to write his account. Let us take a look at it as recorded in the book of Revelation.

Rev 4:1-1.

"After this I looked, and, behold, a door was opened in heaven: and the first voice which I heard was as it were of a trumpet talking with me; which said, Come up hither, and I will shew thee things which must be hereafter. And immediately I was in the spirit: and, behold, a throne was set in heaven, and one sat on the throne. And he that sat was to look upon like a jasper and a sardine stone: and there was a rainbow round about the throne, in sight like unto an emerald. And round about the throne were four and twenty seats: and upon the seats I saw four and twenty elders sitting, clothed in white raiment; and they had on their heads crowns of gold. And out of the throne preceded lightnings and thunderings and voices: and there were seven lamps of fire burning before the throne, which are the seven Spirits of God. And before the throne there was a sea of glass like unto crystal: and in the midst of the throne, and round about the throne, were four beasts full of eyes before and behind. And the first beast was like a lion, and the second beast like a calf, and the third beast had a face as a man, and the fourth beast was like a fly-

ing eagle. And the four beasts had each of them six wings about him; and they were full of eyes within: and they rest not day and night, saying, Holy, holy, holy, Lord God Almighty, which was, and is, and is to come. And when those beasts give glory and honour and thanks to him that sat on the throne, who liveth for ever and ever, the four and twenty elders fall down before him that sat on the throne, and worship him that liveth for ever and ever, and cast their crowns before the throne, saying, Thou art worthy, O Lord, to receive glory and honour and power: for thou hast created all things, and for thy pleasure they are and were created".

The best person to tell us about heaven is the one that came from heaven himself and that is Jesus himself. What did Jesus say about heaven.

In the Lord's prayer, Jesus made it clear to us that God the father lives in heaven. That only his will is done in heaven.

"Our Father who arth in heaven" Matthew 6:9.

Jesus went further to tell us that he came from heaven to do the will of the father that sent him.

"for I have come down from heaven not to do my own will, but the will of him that sent me" (John 6:38).

Angels also did testify that heaven exist. In Acts 1:11 an angel appeared to the disciples of Jesus and told them that "this Jesus who has been taken up from you into heaven will come in the same way as you have watched him go into heaven".

Several people claim to have been to Heaven and back especially in these last days. I do not dispute their claims because God wants people to experience heaven so that they can tell others. Apostle Paul talked about a man that was caught to the third heaven. 2 Corinthians 12:2.

I have proved to myself that the most reliable book about prophesy and the future is the Bible. None of its predictions has ever failed. It is too precious. For the above reasons, I will want to go back to the Bible to give us information about Heaven.

The bible tells us of three Heavens:

1   The first Heaven is what we call the sky that envelopes the

earth.

2   The second Heaven is the abode of the Stars, the sun and the moon. Some call it the galaxies. These are and could be visible to the human eyes through the use of telescopes.

3   The third Heaven is a place of mystery. It is the abode of God, the angels and the followers of Jesus Christ and also righteous Jews who lived before Christ who had passed to glory. It is the location of the throne of God. (2 Corinthians 12:21)

I consciously stated that it is the abode of the true followers of Jesus Christ. because no one can enter into Heaven without Christ. Those who made it to Heaven before Christ were allowed in based on covenant with God. A deep look into those covenants, you could clearly see Christ in them. In these last days, God made it clear that it is only through Jesus Christ that we can enter Heaven.

This may sound difficult for you to believe but it is the unchangeable truth and there is nothing we can do about it. If you think it is a lie and that you can enter by how good you are or by another name or through any prophet, just wait till you die then you will find out the truth.

Our present flesh and blood cannot enter Heaven. Only our spirits or the new body the Christians will put on during rapture of the saints as the trumpet sound from Heaven or after death on earth.

Heaven is a place of our inheritance. God lives in heaven and by the covenant of Christ, we have been adopted and made heirs of the kingdom of God. This makes heaven our inheritance. The bible says that God has begotten us and given us an inheritance incorruptible, and undefiled, and that fadeth not away reserved in heaven for us. (1 Peter 1 vs 3-4). Flesh and blood shall not inherit heaven. Jesus shall change our human bodies into his kind of glorious body by the supernatural power of his spirit. (Philippians 3 vs 21). Heaven is a physical place with mansions. (John 14 vs 2-3). It is a place where our treasures are hidden. (Matthew 19 vs 21). Like I said earlier, you cannot get to heaven with your present flesh and blood.

In 2019, I was in the city of Accra, Ghana to have the heaven conference. A young journalist came to speak with me. He was sceptical when I told him that there are mansions in heaven; not just a few but so many mansions and that Jesus personally told us about them. I even assured him that Jesus has gone to prepare a place for us who believe. The young man laughed and left. The next day, quite early in the morning, the young man came to my hotel to see me. He was weeping none stop. I was concerned because I thought that something very bad had happened to him. I urged him to tell me what the problem is. After composing himself, he went on to tell me of a dream he had.

In his dream, he found himself on a road. On the right were beautiful mansions, such as he has never seen nor imagined. Went on to say that he saw me in one of those mansions and a voice spoke to him and told him to follow me and listen to me. He suddenly woke up. He did not need anyone to interpret the dream to him. he immediately knew that the mansions in heaven are real and that he must do something if he has to inherit one of those in eternity. I prayed for him and led him properly to Christ.

I had another case in Ireland. While ministering I was led by the Spirit of God to tell the people that God is going to visit someone and take the person to heaven.

The next day in service, a family came to tell the church of an experience their son of about 9 years had during the night. According to them, they claimed that their son told them that Jesus visited him in the night and took him to heaven. The boy described the beauty of heaven and confirmed that it really do exist. The parents testified that they do believe their son because they could tell the unusual quietness and peace around him.

There is so much emphasis on surviving on earth. So much talk about how to prosper, kill your enemies, fight the devil etc but less teaching on how to prepare for heaven.

I Corinthians 15:19 warned that: **"If only in this life that we have hope in Christ, we are of all people most to be pitied".** NIV

The truth is that we are the most to be pitied in this our generation because we have put our hope in Christ mostly for what we will achieve on earth without any plan for heaven. Holiness, suffering for Christ and dying for Christ is no longer the teaching of this generation.

Many Christians now see Christianity as a means to success on earth without any thought for eternity. When you talk about

Holiness, the leaders will tell you to take it easy else you drive the people away. Hey tell you not to feed the people with hard bones else they choke. How long will we continue like this.

Let us consider our ways before it is too late.

THE VALUE OF HEAVEN

How can we quantify the value of heaven? The truth is that nothing can be compared to it. If men knew the value and quality of Heaven, they would make heaven their primary objective in life. They will be ready to trade in everything for Heaven including their lives. It is only on earth that we have the opportunity to prepare for heaven. God has given us his Word, the Holy Spirit and the angels to help us prepare for heaven.

Some false teachers have used the value of Heaven to lure unsuspecting people to suicide bombing with the promise of virgins in Heaven. Such a teaching is a teaching that appeals to lust than to genuine quest for Heaven. I have always asked why the rich and leaders of such groups do not volunteer themselves for suicide bombing, rather they send the weak. Don't they want to go to heaven?

Heaven is of great value. It has nothing to do with flesh and blood. In Heaven, we shall be like angels. There will be no marriage in Heaven as we will all be spirits and no flesh to satisfy with lust.

"At the resurrection people will neither marry nor be given in marriage; they will be like the angels in heaven". Matthew 22:30

In Heaven, Saints have the body of the spirit. We will be like Christ. Most people spend their time on earth chasing material possessions. On their death bed, it will suddenly occur to them that they will not be going into the afterlife with their earthly possessions. Solomon came to a point that he was compelled to declare:

"I have seen all the things that are done under the sun; all of them are meaningless, a chasing after the wind". Ecclesiastics 1:14.

To be quite sure of the kingdom of Heaven, you must try to purge yourself of this worldly weight that could hold you down. Paul in the Bible talks about weights and habits that can prevent us from Heaven.

Understanding the value of making Heaven will help you appreciate it. Mathew 13:44 describes the value of the Kingdom of Heaven. Jesus likened it to:

"Treasure hid in a field; which when a man had found, he hideth it and for joy thereof goeth and selleth all that he had and buy that field."

The truth of the kingdom is always hid. It can only be made know by sons of God through the preaching of the Gospel of Jesus Christ. This is made possible by the Holy Spirit enablement and revelations.

The sons of God here mean; those who have accepted Jesus Christ and become adopted by faith into the family of God. This is a great mystery that the ordinary mind cannot comprehend.

When these hidden treasures of Heaven are revealed to a person through the Gospel of Christ, it generates such joy and peace that cannot be comprehended. It is of such value that those that do understand will be ready to let go of every other earthly treasure to take hold of the treasures of Heaven both on earth and in Heaven.

Salvation is a great treasure which cannot be equated with any earthly wealth. It is of such value that the wise will be ready to give all they have to hold on to salvation. Salvation is the key, way and route to Heaven. The kingdom of Heaven is such a great treasure that all should seek.

The joy that the hope of heaven brings is so deep that even in earthly poverty; the joy will not ebb away. Even at the point of death, the inner joy remains. It is a joy like flowing river that bubbles from within.

Verse 45 went further to describe the value of the kingdom of Heaven.

"The Kingdom of Heaven is like a merchant seeking beautiful pearls, who when he had found one pearl, of great price, went and

sold all he had and bought it".

In life, we all have eternity in our hearts. We are all seeking eternity. Many seek for it in different ways and through different religions. Many in the quest for the kingdom of heaven afflict themselves with different afflictions and penances in order to qualify for the kingdom of Heaven. Some believe they can attain it by turning themselves into soldiers of whatever they call God. Majority believe it can be attained through a clean life style. The kingdom of Heaven is expensive and cost greatly to attain. Therefore, whoever finds it, must know that he has found treasure of more value than any treasure in human existence.

Yes, the kingdom of Heaven is so costly that no man can afford to pay the price. Many are seeking it but no man can find it except one seeks for it through the right channel. Let me tell you the right channel to seek and to find the kingdom of Heaven. It is simply through Jesus Christ.

Since no human can find or can enter the kingdom of Heaven because of the huge cost, God in His mercy spoke His Word and the word because flesh and we called Him Jesus Christ according to the earlier prophecy about Him. He willingly suffered death on the cross by laying down His life as a price for us to have access to Heaven. He then made available this access to all who believe in Him by faith. It means that finding Jesus is finding the pearl of great price. Jesus is the pearl of great price.

Your willingness to give everything up for the kingdom of God is what God is looking for. Do you value Heaven more than your earthly possessions and achievements? That will go a long way to tell where your heart is. The Bible says that where a man's treasure is there his heart would be. If Heaven is your treasure or if you are building or accumulating treasures in Heaven, your heart will be there and you will want to make Heaven at all cost. If your treasure is stored on this earth, you will be afraid of death, you will never be thinking about going to Heaven. How can you go to Heaven except you die or change this physical body through rapture?

Many Christians are not looking forward to rapture. They are so earthly focused that they are void of the pleasure that those who are waiting for heaven do experience. The bible says we wait in joyful hope for the coming of our Lord and saviour Jesus Christ.

The hope of heaven generates such joy that surpasses human understanding. Christians are now so comfortable on earth that they have come up with teachings on how to survive on earth. These have crept into churches and have diverted the hearts of the people from heaven; which is the ultimate. Very few churches prepare people for heaven. When you begin to talk about heaven or take measures that will focus men on making heaven, they will begin leaving the church because most of their focus is on surviving this earth. When Jesus told his thousands of followers the basic truth about eternal life; majority left him and refused to walk with him ever again. The truth he told them was:

"unless you eat the flesh of the son of man and drink his blood, you have no life within you. Whoever eats my flesh and drinks my blood has eternal life, and I will raise that person at the last day" (John 6:53-54). His flesh here means the word of God. And the blood means his life which also means his spirit. The gospel of John tells us that Christ is the word of God made flesh. (John 1:14). The bible also tells us that the life is in the blood. (Leviticus 17:11).

If heaven is of no value to you, for sure you do not deserve it. People who have no value for heaven are not ready to die for the sake of making heaven. They do not prepare for heaven. They are focused on surviving on earth. They are very selective of the part of the word of God they want. They would focus on such things as prosperity, survival, healing and ignore such things as holiness, suffering for Christ, loving their enemies and forgiveness.

Is heaven of any value to you? You can start the journey today.

ABRAHAM AND THE FATHERS OF FAITH LOOKED TO HEAVEN AT ALL COST

Abraham saw heaven and prepared for it. Behind the promise of the land of Canaan, was hidden the promise of heaven and the way to heaven coming from the loins of Abraham. In the covenant of Abraham was hidden the eternal covenant of eternal life. Several people referred to as men of faith in the bible were those who saw the promise of heaven from afar and were ready to die for it in other to attain it

Hebrew 11:35 …. **"And others tortured, not accepting deliverance; that they may obtain a better resurrection….."**

Hebrew 11 verse 9-10 exposed a hidden secret of heaven not known to men

"By faith he sojourned in the land of promise, as in a strange country, dwelling in tabernacles with Isaac and Jacob, the heirs with him of the same promise: For he looked for a city which hath foundations, whose builder and maker is God."

Abraham was already in the land of Canaan called the earthly promise but he understood by interaction with God that the real promise is eternal. He was looking forward to a city which hath foundation, whose builder and maker is God. Abraham saw heaven. He even saw the revelation of Jesus Christ as one to come out of his loins. In this he rejoiced. Jesus testified to this when he said that Abraham saw his days and rejoiced. (John 8:56).

Hebrew 11 verse 13 to 16 further exposed that the fathers of faith were looking to heaven and not earthly promise:

"These all died in faith, not having received the promises, but having seen them afar off, and were persuaded of them, and embraced them, and confessed that they were strangers and pilgrims on the earth. For they that say such things declare plainly that they seek a country. And truly, if they had been mindful of that country from whence they came out, they might have had opportunity to have returned. But now they desire a better country, that is, an heavenly: wherefore God is not ashamed to be called their God: for he hath prepared for them a city."

These fathers of Faith lived as pilgrims on earth and their earthly wealth meant nothing to them. The land of promise on earth was not their focus. They knew that the land on earth was a shadow of that true promise: which is a heavenly city.

Verse 13 clearly says that they saw heaven from afar and were persuaded of them, embraced them and confessed that they were pilgrims on earth.

Verse 16 says that they desired a heavenly city which God had prepared for them. They saw Jesus as the way and they accepted Jesus by faith even when he had not yet manifested in the flesh.

Abraham looked so much to this heavenly city that he was ready to go through any test and forgo anything in other to qualify for it. He was ready to sacrifice his only son. He knew the value of heaven.

What are you ready to give up for heaven? What sacrifice are you willing to make? The ball is in your court. The decision is yours today. Don't be deceived by those preachers who focus on your earthly prosperity and ignoring heaven which is the core thing.

According to scripture, one thing is clear, if heaven is your focus, earthly prosperity will somehow find you to enable you fulfil destiny. This also depends on what you call prosperity.

HOW TO PREPARE FOR HEAVEN?

No man can enter heaven by chance. You must be ready and prepared for it. It is not a lottery. It comes only by conscious act of following the laid down criteria and fulfilling the conditions.

1. CITIZENSHIP OF HEAVEN:

The first thing that will ensure you the kingdom of Heaven is the acquisition of the **Citizenship of Heaven**. The citizenship of Heaven guarantees you access to entering the kingdom of Heaven if you continue to retain your citizenship. The citizenship of a country gives you leave to enter the said country except you are denied by the revoking of your nationality.

God has so made it that, the only means to having the citizenship of Heaven, is to accept the covenant of the death of Christ on the cross. One must accept and confess this sacrifice which declares Christ as Lord and Saviour. This confession comes with a scriptural mystery. The mystery is that the moment a person makes the confession and believes it in his or her heart, the spirit of the person is immediately recreated and a new man is born. Once this is done in the spirit, the individual is given the right of son-ship and citizenship of Heaven. It is now left for the person through the reading of the word to come to the knowledge of his or her rights and the use of such rights and privilege.

"That if thou shalt confess with thy mouth the Lord Jesus, and shalt believe in thine heart that God hath raised him from the

dead, thou shalt be saved." (Romans" 10:9)

The bible further asserts that:

"Except a man is born again, he cannot see the kingdom of God" John 3:3

"For God so loved the world that he gave his only begotten son, that whosoever believeth in him should not perish but have eternal life." John 3:16

This must be the first step to Heaven. There is no other way to acquiring the citizenship of Heaven and entering Heaven. Your membership of a church or how good you are is not enough to grant you access to Heaven.

The above explanations cannot be fathomed by human reasoning. It is a faith thing.

Act 4:12 **Salvation is found in no one else, for there is no other name under heaven given to mankind by which we must be saved..**

John 14:6 **"Jesus saith unto him, I am the way, the truth, and the life: no man cometh unto the Father, but by m**

Philippians 3:20 proves that one can be a citizen of heaven by adoption through Jesus Christ:

"For our citizenship is in heaven; whence also we wait for a Saviour, the Lord Jesus Christ" :Phil 3:20.

2. BE WILLING TO ENDURE TO THE END

Preparing for heaven requires endurance. The book of Revelation emphasised the need to endure to the end. Why endure to the end? Endure what?

The Bible tells us that the path to Heaven is a narrow one and few are they that find it. It is a road full of afflictions and requires us to carry our cross and follow Jesus (The Way).

There is this false teaching that once you have accepted Jesus, that you are guaranteed Heaven. This is a delusion. It only gives you access to see and experience the kingdom of God on earth and opens the opportunity to enter heaven. Entering is solely your responsibility through the grace that has been made available. You must enter by faith through the help of the Holy Spirit. You must endure, you must keep away from sin and do not live in sin. If you sin, you must quickly confess and repent. If you pleasure in your sins, there is no guarantee that you will make it to Heaven.

One thing is worth noting. God enables you to endure by His spirit. He makes available all you need to prevail but you must do the prevailing else God would be seen as partial.

The Israelites were delivered from Israel and were set on their way to the promise land. Not all got to the Promised Land but they that obeyed and endured.

We must be ready to get into Heaven at all cost. We must not just accept Jesus alone, we must be ready to endure and enter; for narrow is the way.

" ...strait is the gate, and narrow is the way, which leadeth unto life, and few there be that find it." Mat 7:14

It is like a man who has a passport and visa to travel home but refuses to go to the airport to get a ticket. If such a man stays put, he will never be able to board a flight and will not be able to get to destination.

Many start well in their journey to Heaven. They accept Christ and remain fervent running the race till they meet fierce resistance from the devil. Some give in at this stage. Some even deny Christ and dump their citizenship of Heaven. They no longer see the Heavenly race as a worthwhile race.

The parable of the sower in Luke 8:13 best explains it.

"They on the rock are they, which, when they hear, receive the word with joy; and these have no root, which for a while believe, and in time of temptation fall away".

Temptation is a must and we must learn how to deal with temptation by the word or we would lose out completely.

The journey to Heaven is not butter and bread. The devil will throw everything at you. His hate for you is so strong that he will do all his best to stop you from making Heaven. In return, you have to resist him with all that you have. You have to use all spiritual weapons at your disposal to resist him. The good news is that God has given you all the provisions to resist the devil.

Why is the devil so mad at your attempt to make it to Heaven? The answer is simple. He was kicked out of Heaven and knows the beauty of Heaven. You were created to take his place in Heaven. To add salt to his injury, you were given the power to become a son of God. This mystery is hard for Satan to accept. Satan finds it difficult to accept that man can be called a son of God.

"But as many as received him, to them gave He power to become the sons of God, even to them that believe on his name:" *John 1:12*.

Satan is determined to stop you at all cost. You must be determined to resist him and make Heaven at all cost. Expect him to attack you even in church but do not quit and do not take offence. If you are not attacked, it means that you are no value.

3. LIVE A LIFE OF OBEDIENCE

God is big on loyalty and obedience. Nothing drives away his presence like disobedience without repentance. Obedience attracts him. Satan was chased out of Heaven because of disobedience. Disobedience can rob you Heaven. The disobedient cannot make it to Heaven. Do not deceive yourself that you love God and that you are a child of God therefore can make Heaven while still walking and living in sin.

Mathew 7:21 *"Not everyone that saith unto me, Lord, Lord, shall enter into the kingdom of heaven; but he that doeth the will of my Father which is in heaven"*

The passage above is self-explanatory. It is not all those who say father, father that make it to Heaven but those who do the will of the father. Do everything you can to obey the word of God and leave the rest to God to sort out.

The mystery about the Love of God is that if you are willing, He will for sure give you a helping hand by his spirit. Obedience activates God's favor. The acts of obedience so captivates God that He would make you a promise and seal it with an oath.

The obedience of Abraham to the call to sacrifice his only son so touched God that he swore to bless him. It is that blessing that the nation of Israel is still enjoying till date. Christ was also a consequence of the blessing of Abraham which we are all enjoying today.

"And the angel of the Lord called unto Abraham out of heaven the second time, And said, By myself have I sworn, saith the Lord, for because thou hast done this thing, and hast not withheld thy son, thine only son: That in blessing I will bless thee, and in multiplying I will multiply thy seed as the stars of the heaven, and as the sand which is upon the sea shore; and thy seed shall possess the gate of his enemies; And in thy seed shall all the nations of the earth be blessed; because thou hast obeyed my voice." *Genesis 22:15-18*

In these last days, God has given us an instruction on the only path to Heaven. He has made it clear that there is no other way to Heaven except through Jesus Christ. He announced it in scripture. Obeying the instruction of following Christ as the way to Heaven is the instruction God has given. Those who believe Him by faith prove to Him that they obey Him and He has gladly made Heaven available to them. Refusing to accept Jesus is like making God a liar and it grieves Him.

"He that believeth on the Son of God hath the witness in himself: he that believeth not God hath made him a liar; because he believeth not the record that God gave of his Son." *1 John 5:10*

Conclusively, to make Heaven, one has to be steadfast in obedience. Get rid of anything that will cause you to disobey the word of God. The Bible explained this when it recommended that we cut off our hand if it will lead us to hell.

"And if thy right hand offends thee, cut it off, and cast it from thee: for it is profitable for thee that one of thy members should perish, and not that thy whole body should be cast into hell." *Matthew 5:30*

What it is simply saying is that, nothing is worth more than Heaven. It is better to lose everything on earth and make it to Heaven than to gain or keep the things on earth and loose Heaven. The things of this earth will someday pass away but Heaven is for ever and ever. It may sound foolish to you but it is the truth.

God uses the foolish things to confound the wise. If you have never thought of Heaven, begin to think of it now.

4. LEARN TO FORGIVE AT ALL COST

Apart from accepting Christ, one major command, which for sure, guarantees your salvation, is forgiveness. This seems to be the most difficult thing for most people to accept in a world that is so full of hurt and wickedness; a world where men sit down and plot evil and carry them out without remorse. When they finish their evil acts, sometimes they ask you to forgive them only when they have been caught or put in a corner.

Forgiveness is not an easy thing. How do you forgive a man who intentionally destroyed all your life labor? How do you forgive a man who lied about you and sends you to life in jail? How do you forgive a man who raped you and still mocked you in court? How do you forgive a person that killed your family and let you to rot?

It is difficult yet God expects us to forgive as a precondition to entering Heaven. If you do not forgive, your sins will also not be forgiven. Entering heaven is a really costly affair yet it is attainable.

Mathew 6:14 **For if you forgive other people when they sin against you, your heavenly Father will also forgive you.**

The logic is this, you too have offended God. You have insulted Him, you have robbed Him, you have done everything unimaginable to him even without knowing it, yet He is willing to forgive you. He is waiting for you to ask for forgiveness. The moment you ask for forgiveness, He forgives you without going through your sins or records.

God expects us to do the same. The question is how? He can easily forgive because He is God but we are flesh. How do we manage? The pain is too deep. How does one forgive?

God expects us to come to Him and receive the grace to forgive. He proved it in His son Jesus Christ.

Jesus was falsely accused, beaten beyond recognition, sentenced to death and made to carry His cross. He was ruthlessly nailed to the cross. In the mist of the pain, He had the wisdom to look unto God the father for strength to ask for forgiveness for those that were about to put Him to death.

"Then said Jesus, Father, forgive them; for they know not what they do. And they parted his raiment, and cast lots." *Luke 23:34*

Jesus knew the principles of making it to Heaven. He knew He must forgive in order for Him to make it to Heaven because at that time he was in the flesh. If it was mandatory for Jesus to forgive in order to return to Heaven, who are we not to forgive? God is not a respecter of any man. If He says forgive, then you must forgive.

You might be a good Christian and a good person but if you do not forgive, you will not enter the kingdom of Heaven.

You have trusted your husband or wife and they have cheated on you. You are so hurt that you have sworn never to forgive. Please try and let it go. It is not worth missing Heaven for anything. If swallowing your pride, shame and pain is what it will take to make heaven, then let it be so.

I have sworn to myself that I will never miss Heaven over any person, situation or circumstance. I will let it go and let God be the judge.

As a pastor, I have sown my life into people and they just walk away. Some walk away without saying farewell, others walk away sticking a knife on your back. Some walk away destroying your name. Some refuse to walk away but remain to tear down your work, after which they go rejoicing, yet God commands that we let go in other not to miss heaven.

If anyone is meant to be bitter, I could be the most justified but I can't afford to miss heaven so I just let go.

I read and listen to the testimony of one pastor Ikechukwu from Nigeria who claimed to have died and came back to life after some days. I believed his testimony because there were lots of witnesses to testify to that. One striking thing in his testimony was that at the end of his experience of Heaven and Hell, the angel frankly told him that if the chapter of his life was to close, that he would have had his place in Hell.

Pastor Ikechukwu could not believe his ears. As far as he was concern, he was a good man. He had accepted Jesus Christ; he was a faithful pastor and husband. What was his error?

A day before he had and accident and died, his wife had slapped him on his face. To an African husband, especially an Ibo of eastern Nigeria, that was a great insult. He was so bitter that he refused to forgive her. She tried to appeal for forgiveness but he was too hurt to talk to her. That simple act of unforgiveness disqualified him for Heaven. He was given another chance to return to earth to share his testimony.

Do not compromise Heaven with unforgiveness. Make it at all cost. There is no price too big to pay.

Heaven at all cost. What is your take?

You do not just pray to go to heaven. You simply take action.

The first action is to accept Jesus as your Lord and personal savior.

You can do that by confessing this simple fact into your life.

5. WATCH OUT FOR THE SIGNS OF THE END

Of all the signs pointing to the end, there are a few that we must all watch out for. Why watch out for these ones specifically? It is because these are the ones that can stop you from entering heaven if you fall to them. Matthew Chapter 24 verses 9-13 are too strategic. The truth is that they are happening right now and many especially in the church have ignored it.

9, 'then shall they deliver you to be afflicted, and shall kill you: and ye shall be hated of all nations for my name's sake.

10, and then shall many be offended, and shall betray one another, and shall hate one another.

11, Many false prophets shall arise, and shall deceive many

12, and because iniquity shall abound, the love of many shall wax cold.

13, but he that shall endure unto the end, the same shall be saved.

In our present age, Christians are like endangered species. In the west, they will prefer you talk about yoga, and any religion than talk about Christianity. The moment you mention the name of Christ, people get offended. Sometimes, they get visibly offended and it reflects in their change of color. Christians are been killed everywhere in the world and nobody gives a dam about it. If somebody from other religion dies, it makes headline and immediately investigations are set in motion. This is the mark we must bear for our Lord; to be hated by all nations.

It has become clear that many false prophets have arisen with great signs and wonders. The weak are easily led astray.

Iniquity within and outside the church has become so common that so many people prefer to keep away from church. In the process, they lose their faith and salvation. Iniquity has increased the rate of falling away from the faith. Many Christians have been abused and defrauded so much that they have lost confidence in anything that has to do with God.

The truth here is that we must take the above warnings serious and expect these things to happen. We must focus on God and do not judge God by the behavior of a Christian. We are all flesh. God is God and man is man. Do not let your love for God grow cold because of the activities of other Christians. These abnormalities in the body of Christ are Satan's game plan to discourage you and cause you to abandon your heavenly race. You must be determined to make heaven at all cost irrespective of what presents itself.

The key word here is endurance. In enduring, we must endure to the end. Only those who endure to the end will make it to heaven. Do not be among those that will fall away. Hold on to your faith and heaven will be attained at all cost.

In getting get understanding. Do not die in ignorance. Understand the times and seasons that you live in and refuse to be deceived.

6. BRING YOUR BODY UNDER SUBJECTION.

This is an aspect I want to give attention in my discuss. So many Christians claim to be sure of heaven but are being ruled by their bodies or flesh. Some argue that what matters is for your spirit to be born again. In my studies I came across a statement by apostle Paul in 1 Corinthians 9 verse 27 and it reads

" But I put under my body, and bring it into subjection: lest that by any means, when I have preached to others, I myself should be

a castaway."

The question is being a cast away from what? This statement drew my attention to the need to brig our body under subjection. The above passage raised my curiosity, as one that wants to make heaven at all cost, to look for related biblical verses to satisfy my curiosity. This is what I found:

I found out that when a person accepts Jesus Christ as Lord and personal savior, the miracle of rebirth of the spirit is done. The individual is given the spirit of God and becomes a new person.

The person still has a mind and a body. The flesh and the body is not born again but need to be renewed. At this stage the individual by the help of the Holy spirit is expected to renew the mind and bring the body to subjection. This God will not do this for you outright but will help you achieve it by his Spirit. You have a major part to play.

One fact is that the body and mind being still part of the old begins to resist the new spirit and the new spirit also begins to fight back to control the body and mind. This is where God allows the gift of personal right to decision making to be put into play.

Galatians 5 verse 17 tells us that

"For the flesh lusted against the spirit, and the spirit against the flesh: and these are contrary the one to the other: so that ye cannot do the things that ye would."

That is why you see Christians who have not yet renewed their minds and brought their bodies under subjections sometimes still walk in the flesh. If this is not taken care of, it can badly damage the sensitivity of the spirit and the flesh could rule all through which in turn could lead to one being cats away.

Such acts of the flesh are

" …Adultery, fornication, uncleanness, lasciviousness, idolatry, witchcraft, hatred, variance, emulation, wrath, strife, seditions, heresies, Envying, murder, drunkenness, reveling and such like it" Galatians 5 verse 19-21.

The bible went further to warn:

"--- of the which I tell you before, as I have also told you in time past, that they which do such things shall not inherit the kingdom of God." Galatians 5:21

The truth is that if you do not bring your body under subjection, you might find some of these characters overtaking you and cause you to lose your soul.

How then do I bring my body under subjection of the Spirit so that I do not lose my soul.

The first step is to renew your mind. Romans 12 verse 2 was clear on this issue.

" And do not be conformed to this world: but be ye transformed by the renewing of your mind, so that you may discern what is that good, and acceptable and perfect will of God."

Your mind controls your body. If your mind is not renewed with the word of God, it will be difficult to bring the body to subjection. If you are willing to renew your mind, the Holy Spirit will help you. He will not force you. God wants you to exercise your free will.

Secondly, present your body as a living sacrifice to God. (Romans 12 verse1). This means giving your body over to God to do as he pleases. When you truly do this, God helps you to control your body by giving you the strength to resist the flesh and enforce his will. You must understand that even though you have given your body to Christ as a living sacrifice, you still have the power to say yes or no to the Spirit of God.

Thirdly, you must accept that by your strength, you cannot overcome the flesh so you have to rely on the Holy Spirit to help you. It also means listening to the Spirit and being sensitive to his leading. One thing that you must know is that the Holy Spirit does not force a person. Only the devil does.

Fourthly, you must do this by faith. Everything about God is by faith for without faith we cannot please him. (Hebrew 11:6). You must believe that it is possible to bring the body under subjection by the power of the holy Spirit.

Fifthly, you must take steps not to yield to the yenning of the flesh. You must keep away from things, people and environments that can make you sin. If you have weakness for alcohol, then stay away from drinking places or from friends that drink. If you have weakness for the opposite sex, then guard yourself and avoid compromising positions and places. Kill your flesh before it kills you.

Finally, learn to speak to your flesh. The flesh can hear and will respond to your orders. Refuse it when it yens for the wrong thing. Tell it that you will not grant it's request. As you continue to speak to it, over time, it will begin to respond. The scripture says that you shall say to this mountain be thou removed and be cast into the see and if you do not doubt, it shall be as you say. (Mark 11:23)

One mystery about the flesh is that it knows that it is sentenced to death and that it will not inherit the kingdom of God, so it is bent on dragging everyone along with it to the grave.

Flesh and blood cannot inherit the kingdom of God. (I Corinthians 15:20)

Those who overcome the flesh and are in Christ shall not be stock in the grave but shall ascend to heaven at the fulness of time as Christ did.

You must know for sure that the mind of the flesh is hostile to God and does not subject itself to the law of God because it cannot do so. (Romans 8:5-9)

The flesh must be brought to the subjection of the spirit if you want to be sure of heaven. I am not saying that the flesh may not overpower you sometimes but what I am saying is that you must not live a life fully controlled by the flesh.

We are pilgrims in the world and the flesh wants to keep us back in this world but we must abstain from its lusts because they war against our going back to heaven where we belong.

Beloved, I beseech you as sojourners and pilgrims, to abstain from fleshly lusts, which war against the soul; 1 Peter 2:11

HOW TO SECURE YOUR ETERNITY

This part may look like a repetition but I felt a deep urge to emphasize on it.

Eternity should be the ultimate for every human being. Each person will either spend eternity in heaven or hell. There is no other place. The choice of where to spend eternity is entirely left to the individual. God has given us the blue print to heaven and it is clearly written in his word.

The bible has clearly told us the way and that way is Jesus Christ. He is the bridge between man and heaven. He is the way. The mystery is that finding the way is not a guarantee that an individual will enter. There are a few critical criteria to enter heaven which supersedes every other criteria. Every Christian must pay attention to these.

1. The first criteria to enter into heaven as a born again Christian is forgiveness. As I had mentioned in previous chapters, anyone who does not forgive will never be forgiven. If you are not forgiven by God, it means that you are carrying your sins and therefore unholy. Without holiness no one will see the Lord. No sinner can enter. The good news here is that there is no sin that cannot be forgiven except the sin against the Holy spirit which is hard to commit. Yet if you refuse to forgive others, your sins are retained. This calls for wisdom, for one to be alert and avoid things or people that cause you to be

angry or bitter. It is better to have your right hand cut off than miss heaven. I had also mentioned earlier that your good works are not sufficient. Your anointing and great ministry are not sufficient to take you to heaven. This is a mystery.

2. The second most critical criteria is that after receiving Christ, you must stay in love. Love is necessary to exercise forgiveness. It then becomes necessary that every Christian must continue to ask for the grace to love. We live in a world where iniquity is abounding daily and love of many is growing cold. Do all you can to continue to love. It may be an uphill task but God will help you. One thing about love that will help you dearly is that love keeps no record of wrongs done to it. (I Corinthians 13:1). If you can manage not to keep record of evil, heaven will also not keep record of your mistakes. This also is a mystery.

3. Another critical part in securing eternity in heaven is that you must have faith in your salvation in Christ. The bible says that without faith, it is impossible to please God. (Hebrews 11:6). The thief on the cross had faith that Christ was the son of God and was on his way to heaven. He pleaded with Christ to remember him when he gets to heaven. Jesus immediately promised the thief a place in paradise. If you do not have faith that your salvation in Christ is sufficient, you will not be able to enter. The bible clearly said that the fearful cannot enter the kingdom of God. We all know that the opposite of faith is fear. What it implies is that the fearful is the same as the faithless.

4. As I had previously written, you must bring your body

under subjection and submit to the leading of the Holy Spirit. Like I also had mentioned earlier, the flesh knows it will not go to heaven but must go to the grave so it is out to drag you along with it. It is your responsibility to resist it.

Resist the flesh

" For those who are according to the flesh set their minds on the things of the flesh, but those who are according to the Spirit, the things of the Spirit. For the mind set on the flesh is death, but the mind set on the Spirit is life and peace" Romans 8:5-9.

THE ROLE OF PARENTS IN PREPARING THEIR CHILDREN TO HEAVEN.

As parents we are to direct our children in the ways of the lord. It is not the duty of God but our responsibility as God's fellow workmen. As parents we are caretakers appointed by God to point the children that he gave to us, back to him in heaven. God will hold us responsible for not leading our children to heaven

Proverbs 22:6 **tells us to train a child in the way he should go and when he is old, he will not depart from it.**

If parents take it upon themselves to make sure they train their children in the way of the lord properly, they will most likely never depart from them.

Not many parents know the way of the lord. We give to our children what we have. If you don't know the ways of the Lord, your children stand the risk of missing heaven except they find it themselves as they grow. If you know the way of the lord, please train them in it.

"Train up a child in the way he should go: and when he is old, he will not depart from it." Prov 22:6

Psalm 127:4 says **"As arrows are in the hand of a mighty man: so are children of the youth."**

When arrows are in the hands of a mighty man, he points them on a particular target with expectations of hitting the target. He never misses his target. So we must point our children to heaven and we will not miss the target.

God testified about Abraham in Genesis 18:19:

" For i know him that he will command his children and his household after him and they shall keep the way of the lord to do justice and judgement".

Let God also testify about you that you will command your children to follow him and to make heaven.

As parents, God wants us to tell our children stories of his mighty works. What he has done in the past in the bible and what he is still doing and will continue to do.

When God sent locusts to punish the Egyptians, he told Moses that it should be told in the ears of their sons and son's son. That is to say that we must tell to the ears of our generations to come the works of God. Read bible stories to them, tell them testimonies you have heard and also your own personal testimonies to build their faith.

Deut 6:6-8 *"⁶ These commandments that I give you today are to be on your hearts. ⁷ Impress them on your children. Talk about them when you sit at home and when you walk along the road, when you lie down and when you get up. ⁸ Tie them as symbols on your hands and bind them on your foreheads."*

You must diligently teach your children the word of God. The Jews and the Muslims got it right. We Christians do not take the bible serious enough to teach our children. This bible is life.

Deuteronomy 4:9 reads:

" ⁹ Only be careful, and watch yourselves closely so that you do not forget the things your eyes have seen or let them fade from your heart as long as you live. Teach them to your children and to their children after them."

Psalm 78:5 also reads:

*"He decreed statutes for Jacob
  and established the law in Israel,
which he commanded our ancestors
  to teach their children,"*

God gave them testimonies and he commanded the fathers to make them known to their children. What is your testimony. Let your testimonies point your children to heaven.

STEPS TO POINT YOUR CHILDREN TO HEAVEN

1. Teach them about true Salvation and the hope of our salvation.

2. Be an example by your lifestyle.

3. Encourage them to make and keep good and true Christian Friends

4. Teach them to hate sin

5. Introduce them to the Holy Spirit early in life.

6. Teach them about the link between forgiveness and heaven

Hell for sure will separate you from your children. Not teaching your children about heaven would leave them to the risk of going to hell. If you love your children, you wouldn't want them to go to hell. Hell was not made for humans but for the devil and his agents. (Mat 25:41). It is not a place for your children. If you love your children, begin to prepare them for heaven now.

HOW TO BUILD TREASURES IN HEAVEN

I call this, preparing for retirement. It is possible to build treasures in Heaven. In fact, Jesus made mention of the need to build treasures in heaven where thieves cannot break in as opposed to building on earth where thieves can break in.

Mathew 6:19-21 *"Lay not up for yourselves treasures upon earth, where moth and rust doth corrupt, and where thieves break through*

and steal: But lay up for yourselves treasures in heaven, **where neither moth nor rust doth corrupt, and where thieves do not break through nor steal: For where your treasure is, there will your heart be also"**

The above statement by Jesus is a clear confirmation that there is a Heaven and that it has a location. That treasure can be stored in Heaven for future use in eternity. Jesus went on to point out some features of Heaven in relation to the preservation of treasures. He made it clear that there is neither rust nor decay in Heaven and there are no thieves in Heaven. It means that whatever treasure you have stored in Heaven is safe as there are no thieves to steal them. If treasures can be stored in heaven it could imply that we would not all be equal in heaven. Start building for yourselves treasures in heaven.

THE PARABLE OF THE RICH FOOL.

This is a parable that emphasizes the need not to focus on earning riches in this world without a hope of Heaven.

Luke 12:15-21 **"And he said unto them, Take heed, and beware of covetousness: for a man's life consisteth not in the abundance of the things which he possesseth. And he spake a parable unto them, saying, The ground of a certain rich man brought forth plentifully: And he thought within himself, saying, What shall I do, because I have nowhere to bestow my fruits? And he said, This will I do: I will pull down my barns, and build greater; and there will I bestow all my fruits and my goods. And I will say to my soul, Soul, thou hast much goods laid up for many years; take thine ease, eat, drink, and be merry. But God said unto him, Thou fool, this night thy soul shall be required of thee: then whose shall those things be, which thou hast provided? So is he that layeth up treasure for himself, and is not rich toward God".**

A proper look at the above scripture will reveal a deep mystery about life on earth without the hope of Heaven. It started by warning us of covetousness and the value of real life. Jesus emphasized that life does not consist in the abundance of the things we possess. The things we possess will someday pass away. Jesus saw life on earth as only a fraction of the real life. The real life is in eternity. On earth, most people chase after the material possessions and we often equate achievement with material possessions. What Jesus is trying to point out here is that material possessions have no eternal value. What has eternal value is your relationship with God. Though, we are made to understand that your earthly possessions can be transformed into heavenly treasures if it is used according to the orders and purposes of God.

The story of the rich fool is clear. He is called a fool because he lacked the knowledge of life in eternity and the need to build treasures for eternity. Rather he was busy building treasures on earth without converting them to Heavenly treasures. Are you a fool?

Are you spending your time on earth accumulating earthly possessions? What of Heaven? Pursue Heaven at all cost.

The scripture we read above also pointed out one fact that awaits all men. That fact is that a day must come when your soul will be required of you. One thing is sure; you cannot take your earthly possessions along with you to eternity.

Job 1:21 says:

"Naked came I out of my mother's womb, and naked shall I return thither:"

Ecclesiastes 5:15-16 also says:

"As he came forth of his mother's womb, naked shall he return to go as he came, and shall take nothing of his labor, which he may carry away in his hand. And this also is a sore evil, that in all points as he came, so shall he go: and what profit hath he that hath labored for the wind?"

Why labor for that which you cannot take into eternity. This does not mean that we do not need to work hard but our focus must not be towards accumulating earthly wealth without being rich towards God.

The story of the rich young ruler clearly tells us how to build or store treasures in Heaven.

Mathew 19:16-22 **"And, behold, one came and said unto him, Good Master, what good thing shall I do, that I may have eternal life? And he said unto him, Why callest thou me good? there is none good but one, that is, God: but if thou wilt enter into life, keep the commandments. He saith unto him, Which? Jesus said, Thou shalt do no murder, Thou shalt not commit adultery, Thou shalt not steal, Thou shalt not bear false witness, Honour thy father and thy mother: and, Thou shalt love thy neighbour as thyself. The young man saith unto him, All these things have I kept from my youth up: what lack I yet? Jesus said unto him, If thou**

wilt be perfect, go and sell that thou hast, and give to the poor, and thou shalt have treasure in heaven: and come and follow me. But when the young man heard that saying, he went away sorrowful: for he had great possessions".

The rich young ruler had kept the law. He was sure he was qualified for heaven by keeping the law. One thing is that he really never knew himself. He was a greedy idolater who loved his money more than the kingdom of God. He never saw it. Just entering Heaven is not all. You must also build treasures in Heaven and that is done right here on earth.

In verse 21, Jesus told the rich young man to go and sell all he had and give to the poor and then follow him in order to store treasures in Heaven.

What Jesus was trying to show the man was that his (The rich man's) heart was not right. His wealth was his hidden idol which he was not ready to trade for the kingdom of God. Jesus was pointing out that giving to the poor generate treasures in eternity. This promise of giving to the poor is only for those who have accepted Jesus as their salvation. If you are not in Christ, no amount of giving to the poor will save you.

The Bible argues this when it says that "he that gives to the poor lends to the Lord". Whatever you lend to the Lord is paid back with greater interest and other treasures deposited in your Heavenly account.

We also learn from the same passages that following Jesus is rewarded with treasures in Heaven.

Offering and giving to the work of God.

Offering is a mystery. It is a physical thing that manifest in the spiritual. Every offering is duplicated in the spirit and it turns into treasures that are stored in the bank of Heaven. Offerings, gifts to the work of God, and Christians giving to the poor are also building materials which are used to build our Heavenly home.

I heard the story of a woman who had a strange dream. In her dream, she died and was carried by angels to Heaven. On getting to Heaven, she saw great mansions that could not be compared to anything she had ever seen or imagined. She was excited as she was expected to be shown her own mansion. She was attracted to a particular beautiful mansion. The angel told her the mansion belongs to her house maid. She became more excited and expectant. She imagined that if such magnificent mansion could belong to her house maid, that hers would be unimaginable. She patiently waited as the angel continued the tour of Heaven. She then noticed that they were leaving the Porsche part of Heaven to a less attractive part. She was shocked to be told that an uncompleted and shabby looking house was hers. She challenged the angel siting her maid's mansion. She questioned why her maid should have a mansion and she a shack.

To her surprise she was told that heaven only build with what you give to the work of God on earth. Her maid was a regular tither, giver to the poor and supporter of the work of God but she herself hardly did any of the above without complaining. What you sow is what you will reap.

Galatians 6:7: **"Be not deceived; God is not mocked: for whatsoever a man soweth, that shall he also reap."**

A proper analysis of Philippians 4:15-19 clearly reviews a secret about giving and building treasures in Heaven. Let us read the whole of the scripture for clarity.

Philippians 4:15-19 *"Now ye Philippians know also, that in the beginning of the gospel, when I departed from Macedonia, no church communicated with me as concerning giving and receiving, but ye*

only. For even in Thessalonica ye sent once and again unto my necessity. Not because I desire a gift: but I desire fruit that may abound to your account. But I have all, and abound: I am full, having received of Epaphroditus the things which were sent from you, an odour of a sweet smell, a sacrifice acceptable, well pleasing to God. But my God shall supply all your need according to his riches in glory by Christ Jesus".

Paul was taking about the mystery of giving to the work of God or to the needs of the ministers of God. The Philippians were looking for opportunities to sow into the life of Paul the Apostle. While Paul was in Thessalonica, they sowed several times to meet the needs of Paul. In verse 17, Paul clearly stated that he accepted the gift, not because he desired a gift but that the gift was to be credited to their spiritual accounts.

He called the gift a sacrifice to God with a sweet smelling aroma. Paul was implying that any gift given to the work of God is a direct sacrifice to God Himself.

In verse 19, Paul exposed another mystery and benefits that awaits those who support the work of God. He promised them that He will supply all their needs according to His riches in Christ Jesus.

My conclusion is that every clean and sincere offering or gift we give to the work of God will be recorded and credited to our Heavenly Accounts.

THOSE WHO WILL NOT MAKE HEAVEN.

Like I had said earlier, the fact that you are born again is not a guarantee that you will enter heaven. Not all the Israelites that left Egypt entered the promised land.

Apostle Paul even said that **"those who live like these shall not inherit the kingdom of God".** I Cor 6 verse 9-10

This letter was written to Christians. It means that a Christian who lives in sin will not inherit the kingdom of God. It does not mean that a single sin will deny you. It means that if you live in habitual sin without repenting, you will not enter. Though a single unconfessed sin could still rob you of heaven. That is why you must always confess any known sin and ask God to forgive any unknown sin.

One good news is that if you repent and do not die in your sin, heaven will be open for you. There is a promise in 1 John 1:9 That

"if we confess our sins, he is faithful and just to forgive us our sins"

The Mystery of the above scripture is that God is faithful and will always forgive as he has promised no matter how bad the sin is. Secondly, he is just when he forgives. It is because he is the King of Kings and no one can question him if he decides to forgive anyone. God is faithful and just.

BIBLICAL LIST OF THOSE WHO WILL NOT ENETER HEAVEN

The bible clearly and expressly listed out those that will not be allowed to go into heaven.

1. Those that refuse Jesus as their lord and savior.
John 3:18 states that:
"Whosoever believes in him is not condemned, but whoever does not believe stands condemned already because they have not believe in the name of God's one and only son"

Act 4:12 confirms it when it states

"Neither is there salvation in any other: for there is none other name under heaven given among men, whereby we must be saved". No unsaved person can enter into heaven

2.   Those whose names are not written in the book of life.

Accepting Jesus automatically writes your name in the book of life. The question is, can one's name be removed from the book of life?

Revelation 3:4 **" He who overcomes will thus be clothed in white garments; and I will not erase his name from the book of life..."**

It means that a name can be erased from the book of life. Some may disagree with this but the most important is to cooperate with God to see that your name remain in the book of life. This is achieved by enduring to the end and overcoming by the help of the Holy Spirit.

Paul Said in 1 Cor 9:27: **"But I keep under my body, and bring *it* into subjection: lest that by any means, when I have preached to others, I myself should be a castaway."**

It means that one could be a cast away or removed from the book of life if they live carelessly or deny Jesus.

3. **Those who live in Perpetual sin.** 1
Cor 6:9-11 points out when it declares:

9 "**Know ye not that the unrighteous shall not inherit the kingdom of God? Be not deceived: neither fornicators, nor idolaters, nor adulterers, nor effeminate, nor abusers of themselves with mankind,**

10 "**Nor thieves, nor covetous, nor drunkards, nor revilers, nor extortioners, shall inherit the kingdom of God.**"

Eph 5: 19-21: tells us that those who walk and live according to the dictates of the flesh cannot enter into the kingdom of God.

19 "**Now the works of the flesh are manifest, which are these; Adultery, fornication, uncleanness, lasciviousness,**

20 Idolatry, witchcraft, hatred, variance, emulations, wrath, strife, seditions, heresies,"

21 Envyings, murders, drunkenness, revellings, and such like: of the which I tell you before, as I have also told you in time past, that they which do such things shall not inherit the kingdom of God."

In Revelation 22:13-15 Jesus himself told us those who will not enter into heaven.

13 "**I am Alpha and Omega, the beginning and the end, the first and the last.**

14 Blessed are they that do his commandments, that they may have right to the tree of life, and may enter in through the gates into the city.

15 For without are dogs, and sorcerers, and whoremongers, and murderers, and idolaters, and whosoever loveth and maketh a lie."

I Peter 4:18 says : "**And if the righteous scarcely be saved, where shall the ungodly and the sinner appear?**"

4. The Unforgiving: **Matthew 6:15-16**. This goes on occurring everywhere. It tells how serious unforgiveness is.

[15] "But if ye forgive not men their trespasses, neither will your Father forgive your trespasses."

One major catch in this journey to heaven is the issue of forgiveness. No matter how much you have done for the kingdom, if you die with un-forgiveness, your sins are not forgiven and you cannot enter heaven."

Forgiveness is what every Christian must go and research because it is a key to everything.

CAN THE DEVIL STOP YOU FROM PREPARING FOR HEAVEN.

To answer the above question, I think it would be proper to understand the work of Satan and his agents.

The bible tells us that Satan has come to steal to kill and to destroy.

It further alerted us that Satan is roaming the earth seeking who to destroy.

The bible further tells us that Satan is the father of lies

We also understand that the scripture said that Satan has blinded the eyes of men that they do not see the gospel of our Lord Jesus.

Anyone who refused the gospel of Jesus is already condemned and the wrath of God is in such a person. Men don't just reject the gospel of Jesus. They reject it because Satan has blinded their eyes. In darkness, he lies to them that they are in the light.

When you manage to receive the word, Satan and his agents comes to steal the word from your heart because he understands that it is only the word that can set you free.

The parable of the sower describes such a state as one in which the seed fell on the way side and the birds came and took them away. In the explanation the seed is the word of God and the birds are demons. When a man hears the word and does not understand it, the demons come and steal the word from his heart. (Luke 8:12.) Yes Satan is a thief.

Satan also plays a part in men not understanding the word. This is done through witchcraft manipulations and distractions. The kingdom of darkness is busy round the clock to prevent men from entering the kingdom of God. They see each soul lost to hell as a great gain and a deep loss and pain to God. Satan and his demons have been sentenced to eternity in hell but also want to make sure that they take as much people as possible with them.

The mystery of this is that you can refuse to go to hell by resisting Satan in all his devices. Satan never forces a person to reject God, he tries to convince you and blind you from the truth. The good news is that you can refuse his lies. You can resist him. God has given you all it takes to resist him. Satan never forced Eve to eat the forbidden fruit. He only convinced her and blinded her to the truth of the true word of God.

One other method Satan uses to drag people to hell is to fill your heart with hate and unforgiveness. Hate and unforgiveness is an express ticket to hell.

False doctrine is another means the evil ones tried to steal people from God. False doctrines appeals to the flesh and if anyone falls to it, the person is immediately blindfolded. False doctrines are taught by demons. Sometimes they take the form of righteousness but they deny the power of God in the true word. (2 Timothy 3:5). Satan has disguised his ministers like ministers of light. (2 Corinthians 11:14). It takes discernment by the help of the Holy Spirit to survive this onslaught of the devil.

In these last days Satan has become more sophisticated. He has sent in his demons in millions and his human agents in millions to redefine societal norms and values. Sex is no longer sacred and marriage and family has been redefined. This redefinition of marriage and values is an attempt to bring us to the days of Noah and Sodom and Gomorrah. This is an attempt to force God to destroy mankind. Satan is our eternal enemy.

CAN DELIVERANCE HELP PREPARE YOU FOR HEAVEN?

The above question is something that could raise lots of durst and controversy but I believe I should not shy away from looking into this. I have seen several Christians suffering from strange afflictions that would cause you to conclude that the devil strongly have a hand in their problems.

I had seen very intelligent people working very hard without result. People strongly exhibiting certain behavioral patterns that even embarrasses them. A good example is finding a real born again Christian who cannot control his or her sexual appetite even when such knows that it is a sin. Some born again Christians tell horrible lies only to weep for their sins when they suddenly realized that they have fallen again.

Some try as much as possible to say resist certain sinful patterns but find themselves unable to resist. This has kept me asking if there is any contradiction with what the word says and what is really manifesting. One thing is sure: the word is forever settled and cannot lie.

The bible says that he who the son of man has set free is free indeed. (John 8:36) The same bible tells us that he that is born of God does not sin. (1 John 3:9).   It also tell us that we have overcome the power of sin. If so why are we still struggling with sin?

I strongly believe that many Christians need deliverance and that could help them prepare for heaven. First it is important we understand the true meaning of deliverance. When you give your life to Christ, you have been delivered from death to life eternal. It means that you now have access to heaven if you remain in Christ. If so why do we still need further deliverance? You see, when you take a bath for a day, you are clean but as you walk on a dusty street, your feet gets dirty so you need to wash your feet again and again when necessary.

For me deliverance for a born again Christian is when by the power of the word of God and the blood of Jesus and by the power of the Holy Spirit, you displace those demonic things that may return to have a claim on your life. It could be by your returning knowingly or unknowingly to something that Satan can use as a legal ground against you. The more you consume the word of God, your spiritual neck becomes fat and the anointing breaks the yoke. This is deliverance by the constant study of the word and fellowship of with the Spirit of God.

Also when the word is properly preached under the anointing of the Holy spirit, it could locate you as your spirit keys into it and it could come as fire and hammer to break any yoke from your life. That is to say that deliverance for the Christian can also come by preaching of the word.

When you become fat, the yoke shall be broken by the anointing; (Isaiah 10:24)

Another case is where an anointed Christian by the power of the spoken word commands demonic forces to vacate from a Christian's life and the demons obey and the person is set free. This is also deliverance. The thing here is that the delivered Christian must return back to the word and stay away from those things that easily entangles him so that such will remain delivered.

My point here is that the born again Christian is not possessed in his spirit but Satan could attack the body and mind and influence outcome of things. Most times it is due to the lack of knowledge of the Christian about his or her rights and authority in Christ. I do not see anything wrong in going through personal, general and specific deliverance when you notice unusual things preventing your living a proper Christian life

Jesus command us to make disciples of all nations, and teaching them to obey all that He has taught us. I believe it is in the teaching that we miss it. We bring people to Christ be never really take time to teach them about how to live a real Christian life. They soon digress and fall into the trap of the enemy who tries to claim them back by harassing their minds and body.

Luke 1 verse 74 says

"That he would grant unto us, that we being delivered out of the hand of our enemies might serve him without fear, In holiness and righteousness before him, all the days of our life."

The above verse clearly tells us that deliverance helps us serve the lord in holiness and righteousness before the lord. I hope that you do understand that I said earlier that deliverance first comes the moment we give our lives to Christ, but that is deliverance from death to life. I also said that in our daily work with the lord we need to go through deliverance from the actions of the enemies that had gained root or entrance through our ignorance or that had come in through legality to make false claims to our lives.

There are certain things that I saw in my life that made me go through deliverance and also allow senior and anointed man of God to speak the word of God into my life. I saw great changes after that experience and I received liberty to serve God or you could say that I received the consciousness to serve god more. You may dispute this but I have tried it and found it effective.

One thing I must point out is that one who is not born again should not go through deliverance except the acceptance of Christ as Lord and personal savior.

The concept of deliverance has been so misused and that is why many tend to criticize it. I believe it is effective to prepare souls for heaven. Through the preaching of the word which in itself is deliverance and through studying of the word which in itself is deliverance, one could get rid of those foxes that spoil the vine or those sins that easily beset us and reduces our preparedness for heaven.

If these demonic forces are not checked by the word, they could cause great damage to the life of a Christian and can even cause them to backslide or fall into the lies of Satan.

A good example is when a man who comes from a family with the spirit of poverty. The moment such a one comes to Christ, the person is delivered from the spirit of poverty. The problem is that the person may be ignorant of this basic fact and due to lack of teaching on who they are in Christ will still operate on the old mind set. On seeing this ignorance, Satan and his agents will try to enforce the old act of poverty and play around the persons mind and environment to convince the person that such cannot get out of poverty. With this deception and the individual yielding to the claim of Satan without challenging them, the person continues to experience poverty in all they do.

"As a man thinketh in his heart so he is" (Proverbs 23:7)

If such a person comes into true and anointed teaching on his or right to the riches of God and agrees with it, the anointing can break the chain of poverty that Satan had fictitiously put on the individual because of the individuals lack of knowledge.

In some cases God could open the eyes of an anointed Christian and they could rebuke the spirit and set the victim free. The person set free must continue in the revelation to enjoy the riches of the kingdom.

If the afflicted Christian remains in his or her poverty, pressure could make them compromise their Christian faith thereby their chances of making heaven or even prevents them from preparing for heaven.

One of my major conclusion in this book is that most people are not preparing for heaven because of ignorance. If people are properly taught, they would be in a hurry to start preparing for heaven at all cost. Teaching by the power of the Holy Spirit is key. Leaders and teachers have to start teaching people about heaven and not focusing on making it on earth. If people can really understand the beauty and purpose of heaven, they would make it priority in life.

CAN YOU ENJOY HEAVEN WHILE ON EARTH?

Heaven is where God lives and reigns. Jesus said that "the kingdom of God is among you". It is possible to be in a kingdom and do not enjoy the benefits of the kingdom. Either you are not a citizen or you are ignorant of your rights as a citizen.

Where ever Jesus is, He exercises the kingdom power. Where ever you are partaking and enjoying the full benefit of the kingdom of God on earth, we say that you are in enjoying heaven on earth. This benefits of the kingdom is characterized by righteousness, peace and joy in the Holy Ghost. It means that you begin to enjoy the power of the coming age even on earth. This does not mean that earth is heaven but that you can enjoy the power and some benefits of heaven while on earth.

One thing that is clear about enjoying the kingdom of God on earth and in eternity is that you must first die. The question is, how can I die on earth and still be around to enjoy heaven on earth? That takes me to the gospel of John 3: 4-13. Jesus said that except a man be born again, he cannot see the kingdom of God. Nikodemus in his confusion asked Jesus: "How can a man be born a second time, will he enter into the womb of his mother a second time?" (John 4:4). The message Jesus was trying to pass here is that in other to see the kingdom of God, you have to first die. This kind of death is different. It means surrendering your life to Jesus and let him terminate the power of the old life and recreate a new life in you. This new life is the God kind of life. This process is called regeneration or being born again. It is a spiritual thing that happens within seconds and the life of a person is recreated and delivered from darkness and translated into the kingdom of Christ. It is a mystery that a man can be recreated in spirit. The old man dies and a new man recreated in the image of Christ while the person is still alive. This can only be comprehended by faith.

The moment this new man is created; it has the ability to think like Christ if it so desires. That was why Paul said "..but we have the mind of Christ" (1Corinthians 2:16). The new nature allows Jesus to dwell completely in you. Jesus said that he and the father will come and dwell in you (John 14:23). When the father and the son dwell in you by the spirit, it means that the kingdom of God has come on earth to dwell in you.

It is possible for one to begin to enjoy heaven on earth. The condition being that you must first die. Meaning that the old man must die and a new man created in the image of Christ.

The kingdom of God is not about butter and bread but righteousness, peace and joy in the Holy Spirit. The reason why people do not experience and enjoy the kingdom of God is because they are looking for butter and bread. What they do not understand is that if they seek and walk in the kingdom principles on earth, that every other thing needed will be added. God will provide all your needs according to his riches in Christ Jesus.

RIGHTEOUSNESS

This is the state of right standing with God. In the kingdom of God on earth, the blood of Jesus cleanses you and gives you a right standing before God. In this state, you do not have the desire to sin and if the desire comes, the Holy Spirit gives the power to overcome it. It is a state where you do not enjoy sin and God is constantly pleased with you and rejoices over you. In this state, you find it easy to obey God and delight in fellowshipping with him. This is a state where God comes to live in you by his spirit.

It is in this state that you can boast like Paul the apostle when he said "it is no longer I that live but Christ that lives in me. The life I now live in the flesh, I live by the faith of Christ…." (Galatians 2:20)

In this state of imputed righteousness and righteous living by faith in Christ, if you pass on from this earth, you proceed automatically to heaven in eternity. Heaven on earth is a state of immortality in the spirit. You can only shed the flesh to walk into eternity. People that are conscious of this state do not fear death but see it as a passage to eternal bliss in heaven with God through Christ by the power of the Holy Spirit.

In the righteousness of heaven on earth, you can begin to have the privilege of Angels ministering to you. The bible says that Angels are ministering Spirits to minister to those who will appear at salvation. If you are to appear at salvation, it means that you are already enjoying heaven on earth irrespective of your financial or health position.

The level of enjoyment of the provisions of heaven on earth will be determined by your level of knowledge and implementation of the word. You will have access to angelic host ready to do your bidding that agrees with the will of God. You can activate them in time of spiritual warfare, needs and situations beyond your control. The keys of the kingdom of heaven will be at your disposal and whatever you bind on earth will be bound in heaven and whatever you loose on earth will be loosed in heaven. (Matthew 18:18). You could say that at this state, the man in the kingdom of God on earth has the power to influence the kingdom of God in heaven towards achieving set goals on earth that agrees with the will of God. It is a powerful state to be conscious of. It is experiencing the power of the coming age now on earth. If you want to experience this power, you must get your eyes out of the circumstances and see with the eyes of the spirit and reason with the mind of Christ. If wealth comes your way at this state, you have full control over it because your heart will not be set on it.

In this state of imputed righteousness and righteous living, the Holy Spirit becomes your teacher and teaches you the mysteries of the kingdom of God on earth and how to enjoy them while on earth. Through the word of God, the Holy Spirit begins to teach you about your rights as a heir of the kingdom and how to possess the gates of your enemies.

The more you become aware of the kingdom of God on earth the more you will be able to dominate the kingdom of darkness and also be of great use to fulfil the will and purposes of God on earth.

The Church is an integral part of heaven on earth. Understanding of the truth of the power of the church will help you align with the church and never do anything that would cause problems to the church. Many have made themselves the enemy of Christ by waring against the church on social media claiming to fight for the church. No man can fight for the church. It belongs to Jesus and only him alone can discipline the church and judge it. Consider your ways so you do not write yourself out of the book of life.

If you accept the righteousness of Christ and walk in it, then you will begin to understand what real life and power is. The ignorance of this truth has kept many Christians from enjoying the benefits of heaven on earth.

PEACE

Another Characteristics of heaven on earth is peace. This is the kind of peace you experience irrespective of the condition or situation you find yourself. Such peace cannot be comprehended by ordinary minds or un-regenerated minds. In lack, in poverty, in sickness, storms of life, even at the point of death, such peace prevails and enables the saint to prevail over the situation. The bible called it "the peace that surpasses all understanding" Philippians 4:7. This Peace acts as a guard to the true kingdom citizens in all things. It means it guards the hearts and minds of those who are truly in Christ. It means that this Peace ingredient of heaven on earth is a protective agent against making the wrong decisions or being forced into wrong decisions by demonic manipulations and intimidation. With this peace, you will remain calm and stable in the time of storm.

While on earth, Jesus was enjoying heaven on earth. In the midst of the storm, he was enjoying his sleep. The storm did not wake him up. (Mark 4:38-40) This tells you how deep Jesus slept. He was not worried about anything because the peace of God was with him at all time. It was heaven on earth for him. A person without real peace cannot sleep in the midst of such storm.

We live in a troubled world where real peace is scarce. The world is infested with all kinds of turmoil that so many die out of lack of peace. There is economic turmoil everywhere, war, family turmoil and other social decay in society. Parents are afraid of the future of their children. Life investments are wiped out in a day. In this present world only the true peace that comes through Jesus can sustain a person. The bible tells us that Jesus is the Prince of Peace.

He said that his peace he gives to us not as the world gives.

John 14:27: ***"Peace I leave with you, my peace I give unto you: not as the world giveth, give I unto you. Let not your heart be troubled, neither let it be afraid".***

The peace of the world is always short lived but the peace of God is even unto eternity. For You to experience this peace, you have to accept Jesus as your love and personal savior. When you take this step, Jesus comes into your life and gives you peace and adopts you as a son of God.

JOY IN THE HOLY SPIRIT

"The Merriam Webster defined joy as the emotion evoked by wellbeing, success, or good fortune or by the prospect of possessing what one desires". It looked at it as delight: The expression or exhibition of such emotion. It could also be seen as a state of happiness, felicity, bliss or cause of delight.

It is a feeling of great pleasure and happiness. Joy can be expressed in tears. It is called the tears of joy.

One can derive joy from several things. Money can give you joy. The things of the flesh can give you joy but the problem with this kind of joy is that it is always short-lived.

There is a kind of Joy that is given by the Holy Spirit. This joy cannot be described. This joy causes you to do the extra ordinary.

This joy causes you to stay strong in time of adversity. In lack you still have this joy. At the point of death this joy is so strong that it erodes the fear of death. It is a joy that comes from within that cannot be explained even by the best science. This joy is supernaturally generated by the spirit of God that dwells in those who have become children of God through their belief in Christ Jesus. To continue to experience this joy, you have to remain and live your life in the spirit.

There are several things this joy in the Holy Spirit can make you do.

It can make you leap in excitement that cannot be comprehended even when you are restrained. Luke 1: 41-45 tells us that when Elizabeth the mother of John heard the voice of Jesus the mother of Mary, the baby in her womb leaped for joy.

It is a joy that understands what God is doing even when the person exercising the joy does not even understand why. It is a joy that you cannot control from the inside. It just comes on you. Those who live in the kingdom of God on earth now, always experience this Joy. It is a mystery. Sometimes when I read certain things in the scripture, I find this joy come over me and I sometimes stand up and begin to dance or do some strange things in excitement. It is called the joy of the lord.

Secondly, this joy in the Holy Spirit causes one to burst into a prayer of thanks giving. In Luke 10:2, Jesus expressed this joy.

"In that hour Jesus rejoiced in the Holy Spirit and said, I thank thee, O Father, lord of heaven and earth, that thou hast hid these things from the wise and prudent, and hast revealed them unto babes ....."

Thirdly we understand that this experience in the Holy spirit brings constant gladness. Hebrew 1:9 called it the oil of gladness

"Thou hast loved righteousness, and hated iniquity; therefore, God, even thy God, hath anointed thee with the oil of gladness above thy fellows"

Acts 13:52 says that this extra ordinary joy bubbles in your soul.

" and the disciples were filled with joy, and with the Holy Ghost"

You can see that joy and the Holy Spirit go together. This is a major characteristics of the kingdom of God on earth.

Acts 16:25 shows us that even in the face of prison and persecution, this joy causes us to sing and praise God.

"And at midnight Paul and Silas prayed and sang praises unto God: and the prisoners heard them" (Acts 16:25)

The Holy Spirit enables you to receive the word of God with joy irrespective of your state at that time.

1 Thessalonians 1:6 says **"And ye became followers of us, and of the Lord, having received the word in much affliction, with Joy in the Holy Ghost."**

You can see that the joy in the holy Ghost cannot be caged and enable us to excel above whatever condition we find ourselves.

The joy of the Spirit in our heart acts as medicine to our bodies. It gives sustaining strength and hope in our lives. (Nehemiah 8:10)

We can live in the kingdom of God while in this world. This kingdom runs parallel to this earth yet can influence people living in it, even in this world, to overcome the world. Enjoying the benefits of the kingdom while still on earth is made possible if we live by the principles of the kingdom.

One thing is clear, you cannot enjoy heaven on earth without first accepting Jesus into your life because Jesus is the only access to heaven: be it on earth or in heaven above. If you need to start enjoying heaven, you have to first accept Jesus Christ as your lord and personal savior.

If you want to start your journey to heaven by first accepting Jesus Christ into your life, please repeat this prayer and believe it in your heart and you will become a new creature and on your way to heaven.

"God I know I am a sinner and that your son Jesus Christ came to die for me. I accept Him as my Lord and personal savior. I repent of all my sins. Wash me with the blood of Jesus and forgive me for all my sins. Write my name in the book of life. Thank you for accepting me and saving my soul in Jesus name."

Having said the above prayers, a miracle has taken place in your life. You are now a child of God and a citizen of heaven.

Find a church where the bible is truly preached and start walking with God in obedience by the power of the Holy Spirit in Jesus name.

See you in heaven.

ABOUT THE AUTHOR

Pastor Mike Chuks Nwanegbo

Pastor Mike Chuks Nwanegbo is a Pastor in the Redeemed Christian Church of God. He is presently a Provincial Pastor and the Coordinator of RCCG Belgium Mission.

He is a graduate of the University of Port Harcourt. He also attended the Continental theological seminary, Brussels.

He is the host of a monthly evangelistic outreach called "Solution Hour". He also hosts the Popular Television program "Just Before You go to Bed", a program aimed at preparing souls for heaven. He also Runs THE HEAVEN CONFERENCE across nations with the sole aim of teaching people on how to prepare for heaven.

He is a preacher of the word, a recording artist and has authored several books among which is the best seller "Seeing Beyond the Ordinary".

He is married to Pastor Mrs Boma Nwanegbo and they are blessed with three children; Gloria, Praise and Redeemed.

BOOKS BY THIS AUTHOR

Don't Write Me Off

Don't Write Me Off (I'm Not Finished Yet) is a highly refreshing and moving book that reads

like both a novel and memoir. But it is much more serious and deeper. It is about the ups and

downs, the failures, the vagaries and vicissitudes of the life of a young missionary in the

missionaries' graveyard. Belgium and the ultimate triumph of his faith in Christ, holiness,

perseverance, persistence and the power of prayer in the face of all odds. The book also make

a case for the hopeless in harsh world that does not tolerate or excuse them. It is a significant

voice that deserves to be heard if only for the appeal it makes for these 'reject'. The human

flotsam and jetsam that are crying in every nation, Don't Write Us Off-We're Not Finished Yet.

Healing Breeze

Healing Breeze is what you may call healing made easy. It is the practical application of the word of the God targeting specific issues of life aimed at bringing solutions to them. It is a book that will produce results in your life. If you have never seen the power of God concerning healing in your life, you are about to experience one as you go through this book with simple childlike faith. Receive your healing as you read.

Heaven At All Cost

This book in an attempt to explain in simple terms the need to make heaven at all cost.

It explains the need to prepare and also how to make it to heaven. By the time you are

done with reading this book, your mind will be repositioned and you will no longer be

afraid of death, rather you look to death as a transition to a better future in eternity.

It will also take you away from chasing the shadow of material wealth to building treasures

in heaven for your eternal retirement. If you buy into this reality, you will pursue heaven

at all cost. It will become the ultimate and will change your perception of life on earth.

One thing it will teach you is that there is nothing earthly worth dying for. It will

liberate you from the illusion of making money at all cost thereby releasing you to the

real life on earth and a hope of eternal life in heaven. It is a must read for all in this

generation.

Eternal Enemy

The Eternal Enemy is a proactive book that exposes an enemy that had hated

you even before you were born. This book will cause you to be uncomfortable

and wake you up to the realities of an on-going war against you and society. It

will help you to stop blaming God rather than enlist in God's army to fight the

subtle and eternal enemy of your soul. It will equip you to identify and deal with

the eternal enemy who's only pleasure is to stop you from fulfilling your destiny.

This book will change your mindset and open your eyes to the issues of the

spirit thereby empowering you to be an all-round winner before God and man.